It's Baby's First CHRISTMAS

ISBN 978-1-64300-123-4 (Paperback)
ISBN 978-1-64471-156-9 (Hardcover)
ISBN 978-1-64300-124-1 (Digital)

Copyright © 2018 Leona V. Adams and Mary Garretson
All rights reserved
First Edition

All rights reserved. No part of this publication may be reproduced, distributed, or transmitted in any form or by any means, including photocopying, recording, or other electronic or mechanical methods without the prior written permission of the publisher. For permission requests, solicit the publisher via the address below.

Covenant Books, Inc.
11661 Hwy 707
Murrells Inlet, SC 29576
www.covenantbooks.com

It's Baby's First CHRISTMAS

Written by
Leona V. Adams

Edited by
Mary Garretson

*I*t's baby's first Christmas,
But he's too small to know,
Why a tinseled star glistens
In the candle's soft glow.

An angel smiles down
From the treetop above,
Confirming the greatness
Of God, and His love.

Wee eyes full of wonder
Watch each twinkling light;
Tiny hands fling upward,
And she coos with delight.

Next year, this small one
In a silence, serene,
Will hear the sweet story
Of the nativity scene.

He will stand there, enchanted
By the tinseled star's light,
As he learns about Jesus,
And His birthplace that night.

She will learn, why at Christmas,
Love gifts are exchanged,
To observe Christ's birthday;
Our Savior and King.

A baby's first Christmas --
The sweetest, by far,
Is revealed in the story
Of Bethlehem's star.

In its make-believe fashion,
The scene is the same,
As it was that still night
When the angel host came.

"Thus—it is written,"
That each child shall know,
Why a tinseled star glistens
In the candle's soft glow.

Foreseen by the prophets,
The truth was revealed,
To the shepherds abiding
With their flocks in the field.

How startled the shepherds,
When the angel came down,
And the glory of God
Shone bright, all around.

"Fear not," said the angel,
"Good tidings, I bring—
Unto you, and all people,
There's been born . . . a King!"

God's promise, fulfilled . . .
A Savior for men;
Christ . . . born in a stable;
No room in the inn.

When the angels departed,
The shepherds embraced
That which they had heard,
And then, they made haste;

Found Mary and Joseph,
And the babe in a manger;
Then told it abroad,
To kin and to stranger!

The wise men, with treasures,
Came from afar;
Led by the light
Of Bethlehem's star.

The star went before them;
Stood low where He lay;
They fell down to worship
The King born that day.

They opened their treasures,
Reads the story of old;
And presented Him gifts—
Myrrh . . . frankincense . . . gold.

Having been warned
By God in a dream,
They returned not to Herod
To tell what they'd seen.

"Thus, it is written . . ."
The scrolls are unfurled;
May the light of His star,
Bring peace to the world.

It's baby's first Christmas;
Soon, now, she will know,
Why a tinseled star glistens,
In the candle's soft glow.

About the Author

Leona V. Adams was born in 1914 in a very rural community in Southern Indiana. She graduated from high school in 1932 and wrote one of her first poems for her Cannelton High School graduating class. As a young woman in the 1930's, Leona could have chosen to be only a loving wife and mother. Although she poured herself into her home and family, for her, that was not quite enough. Leona attended business college, and over a forty-year career, she held positions as a court reporter, hospital office manager, clinic office manager, and executive secretary. One of her favorite memories was attending the 1933 Chicago World's fair.

She continued to write poetry throughout her life on religious and social themes of the time. Leona also focused her poetry on the people and places important to her in her life. From topics that included the 1963 Electra plane crash to her family's life changes, her poetry documented the history of her community and loved ones. She also tried her hand at writing songs and freelance short stories. Her self-published book of poetry is entitled *My Inheritance*.

Leona was active in her community as a 4-H Leader and devout member of the Clayton Harris Memorial United Methodist Church. She collaborated with other church members and created a detailed history of this church, going back to its first roots as a part of the Methodist Church Circuit Riders.

Her love of travel included trips to Hawaii, Alaska, Las Vegas, and New York with poetry conventions along the way.

From the Editor

My Grandma Leona passed away in 1996, leaving a family that loved her and was very proud of the writing legacy she left behind. This book is an opportunity to share Grandma Leona's strong faith and her version of the Christmas story through the eyes of a child. For me personally, this book is an opportunity to share the special bond of a grandparent and grandchild with a broader audience. My hope is that this story will be shared in other families and help strengthen their generational bonds.

CPSIA information can be obtained
at www.ICGtesting.com
Printed in the USA
BVHW022138051218
534903BV00015B/64/P